DRYSALTER

DRYSALTER

Michael Symmons Roberts

CAPE POETRY

Published by Jonathan Cape 2013

6 8 10 9 7

First published in Great Britain in 2013 by
Jonathan Cape
Random House, 20 Vauxhall Bridge Road,
London SW1V 2SA

www.randomhouse.co.uk

Addresses for companies within The Random House Group Limited can be found at:
www.randomhouse.co.uk/offices.htm

The Random House Group Limited Reg. No. 954009

A CIP catalogue record for this book
is available from the British Library

ISBN 9780224093590

Typeset in Bembo by Palimpsest Book Production Limited
Falkirk, Stirlingshire

Printed and bound by
CPI Group (UK) Ltd, Croydon, CRO 4YY

for James MacMillan

I shivered in those
solitudes
when I heard
the voice
of the salt
in the desert.

Pablo Neruda, 'Ode to Salt'

CONTENTS

DRYSALTER

WORLD INTO FRAGMENTS

Small breaks first: cup on marble floor,
mirror on staircase, cracked watch-face,
hairlines in roof tiles. Then it escalates.

Plate windows shiver into diamonds,
smoked office towers fold into tobacco heaps,
screens give way to white noise, then blow.

Reasons for this shattering include
too great a tension, too much shrill,
a world more fragile than we thought.

Yet still it goes, ear-splitting, as
great forests disassemble like mosaics,
sugar-glass trees turn shingle, then the sky,

sun and moon as vast burst bulbs,
hot torrential hail. And when it stops,
we see for real, as if through mud and spit.

SOMETHING AND NOTHING

There is a dancer in the woods outside.
I can hear her at night among
the mink and musk deer, redolent
of truffles, needles. No song,
the only sound a twist and slide

of bare feet on the iced leaf-bed,
her breath quickening on the breeze.
Such is her reverie, she has not seen
the sea fold to the icebreakers,
gritter trucks salting the roads.

I hear her even through shutters,
blackout blinds and sash panes,
even through the steady steep of snow.
I smell her sparks on tinder pines,
and I go to her, since I know no better.

SETTING THE TRAP

Tell me, o glass beyond glass, pane beyond pane,
if I make an extra meal, one more cup
for the unseen visitor, will it be taken?

Must I dress it, heavy seasoned, pep it up
with spice and goodness? This is played out
in a small town on the wild east coast, asleep

within its own decline, where fish-smacks rot
on long-dry shores and shadows outfly gulls,
where tide is ever out of sight.

And each night herring, olives, bread, salt, oil
are set out at a table with one chair, one napkin,
left unwatched in case the watching spoils,

and each night after dark the bait, untaken,
is removed, the plate washed, table wiped,
and all the vast and empty sky forsaken.

ANTARCTICA

Is sleeping now, its bright fields intercut with suburbs,
ordered rows of clapboard homes, pin-sharp backyards
all ablaze with jasmine and magnolia.

Its citizens are freer than the rest of us,
living off starfruit from the ice forests, bleached quails
that ripen in the milk-orange groves.

No one sleeps alone here, and only fishermen dream
of wax-white orcas, blind and red-eyed, circling
under ice-sheets swept by katabatic winds.

Of course, this is not *true* Antarctica, where clutches
of tough scientists cross dates off charts. No,
this is *alter*-Antarctica, home to sibling-selves.

Once a month they send a greyhound to the brink,
where ice peters into water. Then the dog pelts back.
The time it takes gives them a reading of the future.

HYMN TO A PHOTO BOOTH

Drag the curtain closed, spin on the seat
to raise or lower. Now a head fills
the oval. Face-to-face at last. Eyes meet.

So stare. Whoever is this? We oracles
do not use names, all answers are generic.
Feel for the point where soul meets skull,

a bone-fuse or knuckle in your neck
that keeps you of a piece. Look empty,
never smile. Border guards dislike

the imprecision of emotion. Face as wintry
landscape. Flash. You have been shot.
Now step out. No re-entry.

All-seeing-I saw ocular blood clots,
sun-blemished skin and a broken heart.
Now wait while I spit out your mugshots.

HITCHCOCKEAN

The birds are taking over. Not in rows on high wires,
chittering on roofs at passers-by, fixing a lone child
with their red-ringed, sink-hole eyes, not by massing

on our window-sills at dawn and tap-tap-tapping
with the urgency, hunger, blunt-sense of the wild,
not with a skirl and swoop like smoke cut loose from fire,

but with a single egg inside each one of us,
lodged in the fold between lungs, not felt until the break,
la petite mort when shell cracks and a song begins,

an airless, blood-borne trill, a pulse, a stretch of wing,
which may be dun wren, bird of paradise, dull rook,
and none of us can know what kind is ours,

nor even know for sure it's there, this skitter,
this arrhythmia, this restlessness, this ache that makes
you walk out, mid-meal, steal a car and disappear.

A PLEA FOR CLEMENCY

Slowly, come slowly, o agents of despair,
paint the skies with portents, number my regrets,
rent me a hotel room, lend me one more night,
let me name my losses, help me pay my debts,
slowly, come slowly, o agents of despair.

Slowly, work slowly, o engines of despair,
schedule in a meeting, email me the date,
time to count the living, time to miss the dead,
let me learn a love song, before it gets too late,
slowly, work slowly, o engines of despair.

Slowly, go slowly, o agents of despair,
bring me lights and sirens, voices in my head,
don't expect a welcome, don't expect a fight,
bring a pack of bailiffs, to shake me from my bed,
slowly, go slowly, o agents of despair.

DERIVATIVES

Upstairs at the Jade Palace: late shift.
Picking at char siu, he cannot find the words,
nor she. Last orders now, so though it's hard
they seek to set a value on their gift.

I love you more than coffee, sugar, salt,
and know that worth will grow. Meanwhile,
underlying assets run to warehouse miles,
and on vast prairies in the agri-belts

pork bellies swing beneath their current
owners, fattened by chutes on a clock,
where vans come once a week to check
the health and wealth of their investments.

Kiss me, she says, as waiters sweep the floor.
He does, then reads a sonnet made for her,
which sounds like one she's heard before.

ASCENSION

Because the sun has a dark heart,
the heart must have a dark sun shut inside,
unable to rise or blaze or set.

Instead, with every pulse, it wanes,
waxes like a pale-then-bold standby
light for some incredible machine.

Because dark has a sunburst heart,
it fights to hold night in: the firmament itself
down among us, standing at a bar

all day with one malt, *midnight*
in a trench coat, bearded, eyes all lid.
If he should blink, turn a lapel, the street,

the town, the day-lit world will change forever:
cobalt, silver, nightingale, cicada,
wolf howls from his mouth, raw ether.

HYMN TO THE DRIVERS

Every second a child is born, a car is made;
knitted together in factory towns
by robot arms with sparks at their fingertips.
The cars wait, possessed but never owned,
left out in the rain, driven hard.

And the children wait for them, a–stagger
on their slow pins, they watch the elders
slide by behind tinted windscreens, lips
in time with the radio. Deliverance comes
as a set of keys and a card in your name.

Even at night, car power is palpable.
Under linden trees they rest on haunches,
colour indeterminate in sodium light.
Think of them as coiled, not cataleptic,
and the road as open, wet with lime leaves.

SOMETHING AND NOTHING

Then one day the world drops into your hands
like a bruised fruit, a-buzz with what you take
for wasps but is in truth all human life.

It trembles with tidal waves and gunshots,
footsteps on the streets of pinhead cities,
a metronomic churn of births and deaths.

At night, it sparkles like a pomander
with billions of headlights, streetlights, fires,
warms your fingers with its love and anger.

You hide it in a bowl beneath a weight
of apple, orange, peach, but as they rot
and purse, this orb just ripens, softens, stays.

The world's sick sweetness hooks your throat,
and all our songs and lamentations coalesce –
a hornet's nest that will not let you sleep.

OPEN THOU OUR LIPS

Because there is a word we must not say,
of course we hear it everywhere.

The dog left in a cold yard sings it.
Unanswered phones in locked houses

are desperate to utter it, newsreaders
with currency updates breathe it

between yen and dollar. Like many so
afflicted I pace the bare boards

of my room and listen to the voice
inside my skull intone it as a litany.

A bit of me is tempted to come out with it,
since none would hear and it would be

a weight off my tongue, but when I open
my window the world rushes in:

moon-lust, elm-smoke, sirens, everything.

FROM THE DEAD

People of the standing pools, rejoice!
The gales are coming from above
to coax and fold the waters.

Watch for new currents in old lakes,
colourless threads like twists
of glycerin disturbing all the green.

People of the scrub and waste,
your votive offerings paid off:
those sunken supermarket trolleys,

bikes and breeze-blocks,
drinks cans and coins, your cat-calls,
mutterings, your drunken o-songs.

So you get your drowned back now,
gasping as they breach the surface,
tearing the weed from their hair.

PORTRAIT OF THE PSALMIST
AS AN OLD MAN

Breathless, in the same chair day and night.
Around him, tissue, tinsel, needles, crumbs;

detritus of another Christmas.
A gale in the alleys and cedars mocks him

with its *ex* and *in*, its surfeit of air.
Except there is no such being as the wind,

simply a transfer of pressure.
Mistral, foehn, sirocco; all projections.

History is like this. *His story is like this*:
blind currents that ruck up empires, eras,

squall them into heaps of leaves.
The frame narrows, stills, on a room

dim-lit by tree-lights on a slow loop,
latchpole pine drying and shedding.

David, king, with lungs like empty glasses.

SMITTEN

Our enemies: we do not like the cut
of their suits, in fact, their very fabric
– linen thick as sail-cloth, white,
but pock-marked as an orange –
accessorised with steel and scuffed leather.

We do not like their taste in jokes,
their labial plosives, their coffee too
sweet and too hot. We do not like
what is lodged in the treads of their boots,
nor the rough tongue of their belts.

Our enemies: we do not like the cut
of their nights, the way they look out
over strong drinks at chiselled mountains,
holding their line against the sky.
And all while our friends are asleep.

O SONG

O spirit of turbulence, terrible name
for a plane, catastrophic tag-line
for a presidential candidate in time

of belt-tightening, name I now give
to what bucks in my head when I think
of my love: the trapdoor drop, shock-live

cable that cracks in my hand, you jester,
you jackal, you careless assassin,
essence of turmoil I plead and I pester

that you will becalm me, as one day
you may; in perpetual twilight, where
rookeries bicker, and three streets away

is the faintest of blackbird songs,
call it an elegy, love once so seamless,
gone to the back of the back of beyond.

SIGNS AND PORTENTS

When all is said and done it's only weather,
but that's no succour for the queues of cars,
burdened with boxes and furniture.

Where are they headed? Somewhere still,
with a mirror lake and matchwood walls,
where winds are tame and sky is pale.

We are the few, the stayers, naysayers,
hoarding meat and bread in freezers,
boarding up the windows, painting prayers

across the walls to *thy will be done*,
then strolling through the ransacked, empty town,
singing in the calm streets *come o come*.

When all is said and done it's just a breeze.
I go on daubing words across my house
to *deliver us from*, then I run out of space.

ELEGY FOR JOHN MILTON

He disappeared in a sharp November,
at odds with England and its gods, the blind
revolutionary and his good old cause
defeated, king in pomp again, *and how.*

Through the open casement in his last hour
he can hear the sellers, beggars, buskers,
dog duets, car alarms, twenty-four-hour news,
evacuations, bomb scares, marching troops.

And beyond the streets, the silent garden
run to seed. Paradise, an old zoo
abandoned by its keepers, broken cages
ravaged by years of unchecked flora:

buddleia, cotoneaster, ragwort,
bindweed, russian vine, dead nettle, ivy,
on the edge of evolving into song.

TO LISTEN

Small hours. The parts of speech
– lost to us in sleep – are found again
in rain outside: sibilants, fricatives, glottal stops,
nothing is wasted. Prayer that speaks
itself (on skylights, roofs of cars,

on nodding leaves). The night sings
in tongues and a black flower
opens inside us. The land lies ever
in wait, slaked but still naked.
And we dream of dead languages,

lost when the last widow – tired
of talking to herself – dies and takes
a lexicon down with her. Listen
to the patois of the dead, its frequency,
the way it maps two worlds at once.

ORISON

Each rescue has its list, as painters knew:
annunciation never simply *girl in a garden,*
winged man on his knees, it needed

comb and needle, lily, apple, mirror, moon.
Beyond the garden, darkest forest,
leaves and branches curling in the heat.

For some, accoutrements are telephones or sun,
a touch, kiss, drink. It may be hard
to pick a moment when you crossed the line.

Yet always away offstage is that roar
of flame, the fuselage of all that's past,
torn open like a blackened wound.

O pilot cast as smithereens, navigator lost
in pine straw. God of rescue, withhold not.
O come. We are waiting for our future.

FACE TO FACE

O glasshouses! We wake to find
all tile, brick, stone released

from its opacity. O engines
of change! Walls are windows.

Neighbours wash, dress, eat
with one eye on each other

in coy and countless liturgies
that echo through the city.

Exhibitionists stand naked,
face their walls and shave.

Shy ones nail up sheets
then watch as they rinse clear.

Now, by night, we move, lie, love
in a galaxy of bedside lamps,

acting out our silent Nohs.

THE TOURISTS

Baedecker's *Eden* guides us, calls it
coyly 'the original menagerie', viz. prototype
of every caged collection. We enter.

Sad o sad the state now: reptile tanks
shattered by flame and frost, great apes
long evolved into salesmen, medics, bankers.

Snow-leopards – a must-see, says the guide –
have seen the lights of town and sloped.
Clouds of birds above, *who never fell.*

Attracted by their shade, I photograph the trees,
rude in their health, flourishing unkempt.
We'll stay to feel the evening cool.

I frame you pointing at the sign-arch
ZOO where one O tilts like a basketball hoop.
We sit beneath a lavish tree, and eat.

SOUL SONG

Did you hear of the man who had
a woman tattooed on his back:
her thighs on his, calf to calf, tapered
down to ankles, heels; her slender arms
etched on the pales of his own, her breasts
beneath his shoulder blades, throat on nape,
her face on the back of his shaven head?

He called her his soul-mate, then his soul.

This is not anecdote, but fable,
I should tell you, *drop the blinds*,
he lay with her ten thousand nights
but she aged with him, blemished,
tarnished, more vascular than luminous
until his true soul, she took umbrage,
upped and left without a note.

PRAISE SONG FOR A BLIZZARD

We give thanks for these vanilla swarms
of fat bees, broken from the future
back to us. Not simply mute, they push
their silence into every corner.
Stings are intact still, but quickly pale.

Once all the swarms have melted,
might a door be left ajar?
Will creatures from the yet-to-be
tip up here, unsure of their footing,
wincing in the slant sun?

A new bird silvers in the black birch.
You tramp through thick snow hand-in-hand
with your descendant, and there's much
to ask, but she is fey and hungry,
and if you speak she will not understand.

HYMN TO NOVEMBER

Strangers are tethered to dogs, or sit
in oversized and idling cars, or bear
heavy coats and bags as ballast.
I keep myself grounded with stones
in my pockets, marked with my children's names.

Yet this morning the city itself
could take-off, under such blind winter sun.
Our words rise up in rapture,
and breath smokes like an offering.
Old stones re-cast as celestial.

Amid all this weightlessness, a beggar
strips in the street, wants out. No one helps.
There is no way to the soul
but through the body. A butcher hangs
a haunch inside his window. *Ave*.

THE ANSWER

When I asked for a port I had in mind a sheltered
harbour: creels, rock stalls, barflies, shanties,
seafood sold from boats and salt-lipped fishwives.
I did not imagine mean streets, blades, illegal shipments,
stowaways, container trucks and cranes.

When I called it a storm I pictured kelp straps
wound on streetlamps, crab claws in the gutters.
I did not describe a house-tall heap of shellfish scree
at my front door, fish-heads in the marriage bed,
the TV an aquarium of shattered coral.

I lift the phone, and hear the waves and seal songs.
Feet catch in marram grass in my front room.
I close my eyes and see a twisted thread of brine
drain endlessly away. This was not the rescue plan
I had in mind. Please reconsider. No, recant.

THE ORIGINAL ZOO

In the long-abandoned zoo, evolution has run wild.
Emperor, rockhopper, galapagos and little blue
are distant echoes in these fins, tails, gills, these minute
bee-tight fish-birds swarming, feeding on reflections.

I press my face against the aqua-tunnel wall,
so thick the glass that all is warped by it, and watch
them swell and swarm around me, darting at my lips.
I wish I could swim with them,

could let myself be turned and turned, give in
to the future and become one speck in a sky-storm,
single pointillist pen-stroke in a murmuration,
impulse inseparable from instinct, choice from gesture.

So I pause, hold my hands against unbreachable
glass and see them flutter at my palms as if I'm offering.
Then before my very eyes they shimmer into smirr.

MENE, MENE, TEKEL, UPHARSIN

One by one, would-be interpreters
are pushed at gunpoint through the hall,
distracted as they walk past rows

of toppled chairs, rioja pools,
half-eaten rolls, concave terrines;
detritus of an interrupted meal.

Led to the wall, each reads the runes.
Some ask if they can
catch this ghost graffiti on their camera-phones.

What we need here is an explanation:
some mineral in the plaster leaching out,
lover's vengeance, rebel with a spray-can.

The words warn what to do, *or not*,
yet within hours the king is dead, his lands
carved up, as meat dries on his plate.

THROUGH A GLASS DARKLY

Mist can be a form of mercy,
all precision gone, all detail lost.

Cataracted hawks hunt woods
for motion-blur, then stoop

into the slipstream of their prey.
I pray for days like these,

when cars are lit cortèges.
As for oceans, fog is respite

from the ache of holding surface
as a clear line named horizon.

Forensic summer gone, now we
live in close-up: flaked face of brick

frostbitten, verdigris and icicles
on statues. A world drawn tight.

Look up: stars are gone. It's just us.

SOMETHING AND NOTHING

Your absence fields are frozen, old man's
stubble punched through soil.
Your silence-scapes echo over oceans,
which – beneath their crash and boil –
hold quietude too deep and still
for any creature, so much pressure
that a man would be crushed to a pearl.

Your breath is held too long to measure.

Your nowhere woods are haunted
by the empty sky through leafless trees,
your scentlessness is hunted
by the breeze, and catches in the craws
of birds that call unanswered,
and wild or feral humans brave the weather
where you will not be conjured.

ELEGY FOR THE UNKNOWN ELEGISTS

They disappear in the dead of winter,
or the high heat of summer, the loved ones,
the missing. And the missing of them shocks
into elegy partners, children, friends.

Suddenly it's all gone: the trees' jagged
silhouettes, the full milk of the sun, sirens
attending other people's lives, and theirs
– the first-time elegists – held in the pool
of a bedside lamp, reaching for the words.

At last, my love, an end to all your pain,
in angels' arms until we meet again.
Couplets for the evening paper, letters
with no address, tucked in family Bibles.

Outside, elsewhere, roadsides bloom with rude health:
wreaths of fuschia, wood-sorrel, willowherb.

THE DARKNESS IS NO DARKNESS

It has no fabric, neither cloak nor hood,
leaves no trace on tongue or fingers,
powder, scent of lilies, damsons: nothing.
True dark would be coarse-grained, clotted,
dense enough to bear our weight,
deep and dazzling, but the most we get here
is mere taper, snuffed, kept in attic rooms
against its will, fugitive beneath banked snow,
lost in twists of cave. Yet if there is in this

no fear, how come I wear a tight and light-less
suit all day between my skin and clothes?
Call it a superstition, like a shark's tooth hung
around the neck, bear claw in pocket.
I wear my cure-dried hide of absence,
so darkness will take me for one of its own.

DISCOVERERS

What vexed Vasco da Gama after weeks
of river giving onto river – *Oscillano, Awdl, Baga* –
name breaking onto name, tracing delta, tributary,

hacking through jungle and scrub to the source
of this great rush of water from which eels,
clean clothes and death are drawn each day;

what really wounded him was when he traced
it to a tap in the backyard of a bombed-out bar.
His heart broke as he paddled through the gutters

of this ghost metropolis. Picture Vasco:
boots bestriding flagstones cracked beneath
the tap which whistles as it spits.

He thinks there are two kinds of people:
one would turn the tap off, the other wrench it full on.
So he took a drink, and knew which one he was.

EXCISE ME

So shattered is my heart from endless
pounding at my chest wall to get out,
that I give in one summer dawn and cut
then lift it. Cupped in my hands
like a half-caught bird, it cools and stills.

I place it on the sill to keep it warm,
and lie down on my bed to take stock
of this new thoracic calm. Hours pass,
then weeks. The sun through glass
dries my heart into a peach stone.

Another day, I think, just one more
to be sure I will recall this stasis so deep
I can hear huge clouds of blind fish
under ice-sheets, spiders in the leaf-mould
of distant forests, your thoughts.

HYMN TO A TOLBOOTH

She has my coins but still the bar stays down.
I tap the wheel and rev then glance behind,
a queue of drivers curses at my back.

She has my toll but will not give me green.
My window's down but hers is up and locked.
Her head's stuck in a book and nothing moves.

She has my future in her white-gloved hands.
If I can join the tail-lights on that bridge,
then I will taste new life across the bay.

She has me in a hold and will not loose.
The cars behind peel off to other lines,
but she and I are not done with this yet.

She has *The Wild East* written on her book.
Her uniform is hot, the river cold,
and I am held fast here between two lives.

THE FORTUNE-TELLING RABBITS OF ISTANBUL

are calm now, in the midday burn, their owner
smoking as he shuffles colour-coded cards

on which are written slants and intimations
for the backpackers who queue up at this stall:

you face one obstacle, that's all, then riches fall to you,
or that old staple *you have two secret admirers.*

So these dead-eyed seers sniff the paying hand
then lift a card between their teeth, as if to prove

a link between the stench of sweat and coins
and one of fifty futures summed up in a line.

And as they pick out mine I think I catch a spark
behind their pink eyes and I know they see

my road ahead: spill of oil, old slow hind, swerve.
Mute harbingers, I'd like to wring their necks

but first another coin, another card, another chance.

ON EASTER SATURDAY

Hell is being harrowed as we speak,
ten thousand leagues below us a colossal fish
with xylophonic teeth is filleting the deep,

and in its wake comes all this:
blossom pulls from orchards, streams from peaks,
the sun – though weighted by the days

it freights inside – is drawn into a lake
and hauled down to the darkest ocean trench,
since depths are being harrowed as we speak.

And though I know it makes no sense,
I feel – if I stand still – its tinfoil scales, the blinkless
eye, the muscle of its tail, and all that I once

took as mine is flensed from me, a thankless
healing, leaves me wondering if I am sea, or fish,
if harrowed hell is me, if I am cursed or blessed.

SMOKE

First one tree, then another, horizons close
towards us, house-lights dim and drown.
The huge, low moon dissolves. Pray in us,

spirit, animus, holy ghost among
the wet leaves, in the smoke's mute song.
Eyes sting. All perspective gone.

One building bleeds into another.
Torch beams shrink to yellow burrs.
Headlamps fade to dandelion clocks.

Distances collapse. Shouts could cross
streets, valleys, oceans. Silence, broken
by a siren on another continent.

And what burns? Sweet and salt,
bracken, berries, hair. What new edifice
hardens within, waits for the world to sharpen?

WE DO NOT KNOW THE DAY

Outdoors is lost in this drench;
all the edgelands (scrapyards, scrub,
freight yards stacked with wet cars)
has become a waterglass metropolis.

Within today's unceasing rain,
countless beaded rooms await us –
every size from concert hall
to sentry box, but all without a ceiling.

So the restless try these rooms
to see what fits: a crystal skyscraper,
up-ended coffin in the middle of the road;
these are not the many mansions

we were promised, merely mock-ups,
dry-runs of a city yet to come,
torn up by a passing car.

THE ORIGINAL ZOO

Along the rows of habitats we file:
bare tanks with sand, bleached branches,
cages run rampant with weeds,
rope swings for those long in arm and tail,
fenced-off copses for pack-hunters,
box rooms with unmade beds,
kitchens with unwashed plates and knives,
high-rise apartments and boardroom
tables with the meeting notes half-done:
we base our estimates on current trends,
a cup and saucer with the tide long gone.

And all along we look the harder at
each micro-climate, waiting for a flicker in
the leaves, a cough, a call, some sign that we
might match the brute strength of our homes.

DESERT HERMITS

A brace of greyhounds slinks across
a whitewashed yard in search of shade.
Bougainvillea swoons, walls ablaze.
Air-con units hum their vigil,
cameras glaze as petals falter.

The dogs' man reads *Exodus* and dozes.
His eyes are pinched as pinholes.
Flies, made swift by natural selection,
stipple him. His pool filter sucks
and gibbers. He never learnt to swim.

There are cacti where the trees should be,
swagged with cobwebs thick as nets.
His demons fatten in the heat –
sluggish koi at the deep end of his pool.
His freezer fills with manna.

THE OTHERS

Other people wake up, wash, blink out at icy
wastes or plumes of steam.
Some are scared by what they have to do today.

They dress in other people's many ways:
shirt first, shirt last, no shirt at all.
And some resent the clothes they have to wear.

If you were there to see them, you would mark
the way they thread their buttons through,
the moue they give the mirror as they leave.

Thoughts of other people are opaque,
the weather in their souls a mystery.
Some, from restive nights, are slow to rise.

Being other, they have not met you yet,
but some – with time and chance – could love you,
if you would let them get that close.

THE COUNT

Born with a ration of heartbeats,
we should eke them out, walk the shores
of great, still lakes and tap their wells.
Trees should be our mentors, tall ones
where the crown lolls like a cowl.

We could learn from astronomers,
breathless on the high plains where the air
is clear: tilting huge scopes
at scattergrams of long-dead suns,
tracing patterns among the crystalline.

Or a pearl diver with swallowed breath
and heart rate halved, combing beds of weed
in search of abalone, urchin, unaware
that when she surfaces she is the last soul left,
the rest of us spent up and gone.

THE SCENT

Before she boards the last train lit
and waiting, first she fills a basin
in an empty washroom, rinses
his perfume from her face, hands, neck,

then sends him spiralling from
porcelain to lead, to earth, to stone.
O oceans, bear him to your breast . . .
then out beyond the breakers

where, unmanned, ungoverned sea
teems with switchback shoals,
and gannets pitch against the wind.
She wears his absence like a scent.

Hours away, he finds a hair of hers
stitched into his shirt like fuse-wire,
though he will later tell her *like brocade.*

DES CANYONS AUX ETOILES

For all we know the canyons and the stars
could be in love tonight, gazing at
each other for the first time without fear.
Worlds apart, their act of love is delicate:

a pale simple glow on desert rocks,
the touch of shadow on a dying sun,
gentler than the love of moon for lakes,
which leaves its imprint on them as a burn.

For all we know the snakes and scorpions
that soak up canyon shade are twinned
with luminescent opposites above, in
a long, slow dance on cooling sand.

Some nights it helps, to picture stars
seducing canyons as we lie out alone,
even though we know the dance must end.

PORTRAIT OF THE PSALMIST IN
MID-LIFE

Parked up on a hill of purple lupins,
he gazes out across a desert, taking stock,
an inventory of the life so far, his big career,

the sheer number of times you could
circle the earth with a belt of words
from the hits he has written and sung.

Then there's the battles, the odds
overcome, plots uncovered, giants slain,
the graft and sacrifice, all that.

His phone rings – a wild-west campfire
pastiche tune - says *caller withheld number*.
But he listens: *This is a recording, but it's free.*

*Do not hang up. If you have debts there is
a quick and painless way* . . . He cuts it.
What is debt but riches on account?

PORTRAIT OF A SKULL

The skull beneath the skin is sick
of leaching through the sallow cheeks
and sockets of lost children or old drunks.

What about, it pleads, *my effortless
postpartum plate tectonics, unfurled
origami, grapefruit with a thumb-press pulse.*

And what about its role as thought-keeper,
guardian of memory, goldfish bowl
where words can feed and grow?

But no. It's all memento mori,
dental battlements and sordid stories
told by archaeologists about a life

of brutish brief excess: impacts, contusions,
always with that gormless rictus grin.
So keep me under skin, or you'll be sorry.

PASSOVER

Why is this night different? I'll tell you:
a second moon looks down on us, the same
size as the one we know, but inverse,

so instead of pewter, cratered, it is blue-black,
satin without blemish; no seas, no peaks.
Sleepless separated lovers take sad steps

on balconies or piers to gaze at moon-mark-one,
but centuries of poems, oaths and dances
could not rescue it, so now it hangs,

waxen in the star-tree like fake fruit.
The change is slow but sure:
a tide pulled out too far, a broken vow,

a habit unrehearsed, a shift of power,
and slowly our allegiances have changed,
the firmament more full, and not so clear.

IMMORTAL, INVISIBLE, WISE

In such mighty stature he stands,
or rather, he towers above what passes
for a plain here. And he holds so still,
has held so long this, his repose,
that no one sees him any more.

In plain air vanished, taken for
cumulonimbus, escarpment, cooling tower agape.
He has become no more or less than sky.
Pylon skip-ropes swing between his feet,
airliner wing-tips brush his lips,

the sun's print in his eye becomes
a day-lit pole-star, and although the world
is never silent, there are split-second
gaps when you can hear his long-drawn
breath begin to shape a word.

ANIMAL OF LIGHT

That instant, in the *Hotel Splendide*, when you
pulled the cord to let that high window
help you find your earrings, button up your dress,
you loosed into our room an animal of light,
a filament so fine and quick you never saw it.

One blink, ill-timed, and I had lost it too.
I know it came to search us, and to show
us what we kept unlit, the bruised fist
of the heart, its inner walls a cave-art
record of the beasts that make us hunter, hunted.

Elver-slim it slid beneath my skin, rifled through
the pockets of my lungs. I coughed, but no,
it would not let me be. Worlds away from this,
a dog waits in a cold hall, finds the one bright
square of sun on tiles, and sleeps in it.

THE NIGHT PORTER'S PROMISE

Guests returning late will get a clipped *Goodnight*,
a blind eye turned towards that mystery companion.
Tables will be laid for morning's conference: clean cups,
name-tags, branded pens and pads, a whiteboard
for the *Top Ten Sales Techniques*. Beauty, solace
I will find in details: catch of till-screen light
on bottled spirits fat-necked in their optics,
swags of laundry-ready sheets like shucked shrouds,
steady hum of air-con's flight through tranquil skies.

I pledge to greet the rows of shoes left out to polish,
with alacrity. I undertake to steer *Hotel Splendide*
through territories of darkness without loss or lack.
I swear on the guest-book to lay newspapers
at every door and waken no one, then to stare
into the silent hours, until the silent hours stare back.

FIN DE SIÈCLE

A few more mosquitoes than usual
rim the cups in pavement cafes,
fleeter, sleeker, bred to dodge the swats.
Seal all the gaps you want,
they still get in.

Where was the line crossed
from age to age, world to world?
A down-and-out lifts the body
of a dove from the gutter,
wraps it – warm bread – in yesterday's paper;

he, without knowing it,
ushers us in.
Which brings us to grace,
and a waiter who shines a cracked glass
then offers it up to the window.

AFTER A LINE BY GEORGE SEFERIS

The time came, and the dogs tore him to pieces.
Or it came and they rested their muzzles on his lap,
or it came with such stealth he slept through it.

Hindsight favours what becomes, and the past
concurs, shrugs into line behind the love affair,
the sickness unto death, the sudden lapse,

which now must seem inevitable, ever there,
the way a swift incursion in the night will show
that your city lay as open as a split fig.

And the hounds, those feral packs that took their cues
from fate, and did its work, primed to rear up
at a finger-snap, mere bone-meal now.

Euripides, whose throat we hear they tore,
was killed by winter's chill, betrayal, long before
the dogs burst from their dark, wet groves.

NIGHT FREIGHT

Our goods – in transit as we sleep –
are boxed to ride the rail-tracks, oceans,
new roads cut by truck-lights, all to keep

the pledge they make to come into our homes
and shine. *Our chattels, may they bless us.*
But the house of night has many rooms,

and many other kinds of solace.
What are ghosts but roads not taken,
selves that never made the flesh,

bled through from dimensions
too close and too subtle for our senses.
I lie awake and count missed chances one by one.

What gives the real such precedence?
Without strong shades, hard lines, it has
no edge over the undone, all the absence.

WHOSO LIST TO HUNT

Six white hind staggered to a forest's edge
one winter dawn and stepped into the open,
dazzled after roaming no small age

under the oaks' and elms' protection,
so we took them in, tended to their sores
then fed them up on snowberries and sun.

Diamonds on their necks pricked out words
in a long-stilled tongue, which scholars read
as: *Do not touch us, we are Caesar's.*

Gaze into their eyes, you feel their need
of comfort, contact, yet there is no way
to tell them that their king is ancient dead,

his palace a museum. Such raw loyalty,
such foolishness. Even now they flinch
when touched, paraded through our cities.

YOUR YOUNG MEN SHALL SEE VISIONS

O mother of beauty, the simple boy who said
he saw you − who ran into the dining-room and fell
to pieces, who made the diners spit into their soup −
before he fell I knew it was my duty to record
his eyewitness account, to wit:

Against the banks of snow and ice, beside
the rose-wall, well beyond the *Hotel Splendide*'s earshot,
there he found you, wounded by the world's griefs,
shimmering. Your body, yes, your flesh made
his creep out of terror and desire. *What shape?*

I asked. *What form of body?* But the more he said
the less he knew. He lay in rapture, glazed eyes
and St Vitus' tongue. Why did you choose
a messenger so unfit to bear truth, the single truth
we had to hear, o mother, o mother of beauty?

THE RECKONING

The days line up outside,
shuffle on the gravel to a hissed command.
All this in the dead small hours, when lack of heat
makes them transparent, so I lift
the blind and see a land out for the count:

plane trees, parked cars, bins, one cat,
a ghost of days, my days, in rows
too indistinct for me to number them.
I'm back in bed, but sleepless.
What are they rehearsing?

Can we not, I want to shout out of the window,
play this by ear? Instead,
I tune the bedside radio to shash,
faint morse taps, drifts of foreign ballads,
to keep the days at bay.

A DOG HEARD BUT NOT SEEN

Utterly alone, it barks through the night
in a backyard across town, and steals
your sleep from you. As respite

from the future and its fears, you call
the roll of enemies, friends, lovers
and pray for them, then one-by-one hold

each up to your inner light, until a face comes clear.
You pray it matters to be held so still,
and that someone holds you somewhere.

The dog begins to holler like a wolf,
then silence overwhelms it, and it stops.
Absence seems a presence in itself.

All the while I'm lost to you in sleep,
I am not with you when you need me most.
And the climb to dawn is long and steep.

WHAT THE NIGHT TOLD ME

Three hailstones from a blameless sky:
the first, it wakes me, scutters on my roof,
the second shivers down my spine,
the third falls in a field and leavens.
End of story, end of storm. *Recount.*

Awoken by a clatter, restless sleeper, I
went out to look for prints of devil's hoof,
when an ice-fly scored a red line
from my collar down my back. O heaven,
hot, still firmament, how ice? *Recount.*

I woke because I heard a cry.
I stepped outside to look for proof.
The cry, the prints, the hooves were mine.
But land was deep, crisp, even,
and all the world was hale. *Recount.*

PORTRAIT OF THE PSALMIST AS
A MAN IN TEARS

Or rather, after tears, when all is spent,
the bedroom marinated, pools and towels, mist.
And mister lachrymose, the cry-king, back
inside his childhood body, clearer, cleaner,
fit to dash full-tilt across an open field.

Now look, his old self says to him, *there's milk
in the refrigerator, winds in pines outside,
a list pinned-up with all the tide-times.
Seize the day, the gift those tears have left.
Try not to make the same mistakes again.*

So he stands in the hallway and is calm,
the powders of his fear too damp to light.
And for the first time yet he sees the bones
that form his soul, a skeleton so strong
that he could, *does*, leave home and start again.

WHAT IS WRITTEN

Behind the badge on his shirt
each player has the word *believe*,
and when he scores he kisses it.

Conscripts carry letters from a lover,
stapled to the heart-side
of their vests to keep their hopes alive.

A bad judge writes in blood-red
ink across the inside of the sun visor
in all his cars *the law is good*.

I can't read faces any more.
The ones that pass me on the street
all look identical, all strangers.

I stare too long, stay up too late,
try thicker glasses on
to read the subtext of the night.

HIRAETH

You know that sense of homesickness? Here's why:
late evening, in the kitchens of *Hotel Splendide*,
a commis chef was practising his crème brûlée
and dropped the torch, which lit a cloth
hung on his belt, which tripped the heat alarms.

The car park filled with shivering guests,
then rumours and a racket spread, until all over town
the frightened took to streets in flight from unseen fires.
Contagion seized the wires. Within weeks nations
camped in forests; fleeing radiation, plague or freeze.

They tried to build their lost towns somewhere else,
in exile until wild was home, and new was old.
Even now, when we turn to mount a step that isn't there,
reach for a door and meet a wall, we sense the maps
of those still empty towns are written in us.

HYMN TO THE FACES

A wall of photographs from nowhere,
overnight gallery of wide-eyed mugshots fills
the side of city hall. Whoever did this
took ten hard hours, ladders, nails, a spirit level.
Now it looks as though the wall before was naked.

Patient queues are forming: mothers, brothers,
guards in tired suits, hunched grandparents
scan the rows they cannot reach. Some cry for
what they find or don't: missing, late, wanted.
Early sun, unhelpful, blinds the gloss surface.

Steam lifts from grids, cables warm. Someone
works to keep this city live while the ritual plays out.
No one dares say what they all think:
These are just shapes on squares of paper.
This is not my son, and this is not my daughter.

PORTRAIT OF THE PSALMIST THROUGH HIS BEDSHEET

Some king this sun-king; less majesty, more mound,
under the covers for days in denial of daytime,

his bedsheet – a relief map of his grief – a shroud
tight round him streaked with jizz, sweat, grime,

tears, nightmares, screams and prayers; one hand
stuck out, belly-up with broken nails, a plate

by the bedside untouched, a mind unsound.
And all the while they wait outside, shift foot-to-foot:

prim bankers to say he has none left to spend,
his past, with a list of sins in its blazer pocket,

destiny – thigh-boots and beehive hair – keens
at the door with her sorrows and fears. *Shut them out.*

One day, he prays, one dawn soon he will unwind
the sheet, hold it up like a photographic plate

and read the reckoning of what was done and felt.

NIGHT TRAIN

Lit not so she can see to clip our tickets,
nor so we can read the news, but lit
to make of us and it an eel-shaped full

vivarium to show the wild hills what
a world can be. And I would like to say
our thoughts, as passengers, crack

between us like a static cloud, and *soul*
means a million points of interconnection
and bind, but none of this is true tonight.

Instead, the slow fields, level-crossings,
tight, grey farmsteads hear and miss us,
passing like a single slub of thought

from south to north, slowest synapse ever,
one idea, say, *life as journey*, fading
even as it bears us, and silence in its wake.

THE ORIGINAL ZOO

I remember *Fruit Bat Forest* by repute:
a hangar sealed round perma-night,
equatorial and fetid, thick with insect clouds
that hide the Livingstone's, Rodrigues, Seba's
endless loops of flight, loquacious
at a frequency above us.

Now we steel ourselves to witness
what this jungle has become since last we looked.
I imagine bats evolving down
and out, grown fat on windfalls, idle, wingless,
fighting for floor footage with distended
spiny mouse and hissing cockroach.

Instead, we find darkness is not darkness,
but a son et lumière, the bats reborn as beasts
of light, high above the stench of rotten fruit.

LUPINE

Cry one wolf, now cry two, three,
until a whole pack sings up skywards.
I would call it prayer, were this some

frost-seized forest, dense and wild,
hard weeks' walk from the nearest road,
where spring and summer never come,

where birds are flightless with the cold,
and spruce-sap toughens in the rind,
where trees can fall and no one hears.

But this is a metropolis, full human:
summer's shimmy, lazy parks, slow roads,
business breakfasts, bears and bulls.

Take to the hills, I think they cry, or *streets*.
We thought they were our pets.
Their pack-sense never smelt like this.

POEM FROM A LINE BY OSIP MANDELSTAM

Now I'm dead in the grave with my lips moving.
O, the respite, the cold clutch of earth,
and above me the world in high summer.

The fact that I loved needs no proving,
so why do these love-lines still rattle my teeth?
All of my unsaid the earth lets me honour,

muttering it to the worms. And I'm losing
my grip on the reason I speak all this truth
about life as I lived it, the pity and clamour,

heartbeats I spent when I should have been saving.
Now I'm meat on the turn, save my jabbering mouth:
the old jokes, the gossip, all lisp and stammer,

slang-licks, torch-songs of passion and grieving,
emptying out to the last wisp of breath.
O rot, take my lips till I'm sweeter and dumber.

GUILD OF SALTERS

Years of working with the white
marked them for keeps;

faces drawn like tight masks,
cheek-skin you can strop a razor on.

Walking desiccants,
they serve us at the edge of wakes,

at bedside vigils when words fail.
Put one in a room,

and drinks unsweeten,
jokes get subtler.

But the price they pay puts me off:
sandpaper for eyelids,

thirst that never pales,
ingrown lips and tongue as biltong,

so their only solace is the sea.

THE LIMB THAT CARRIED EVERYTHING

I wake to find my arm
curled like a lame wing across me
– a collapsed embrace – with her,
the one I held for so long, gone.

And I hear her downstairs,
coaxing slatted sun between blinds.
Dead arm, are you rehearsing loss?

Or rather, have I carried contraband
– a child, a name, a landscape –
through light years of dark, and now, slug-limb,

you rest while other sleepers bear it,
a relay through endless rooms?
I'm glad, in lieu of weight, to have
this ache and weakness.

PORTRAIT OF A DOVE

The dove of peace is sick of being a symbol,
longs to pick fat sunflower seeds
from pots on Spanish balconies. *Paloma*
wants to stuff her crop
with bin-ripe chilli-chicken-wings.

She yearns to burst the white chest
of a fan-tailed pigeon with a well-aimed nod.
She blames Picasso, him and Noah,
for her life of limit, though she may
– with her melting burr and trill,

head on tilt – have backed her way into it.
Now, as dusk draws a threnody
from high in a lemon tree, she does not
sing for shattered cities, but her own
nut-hard and ever tightening heart.

A PLATE FOR A FACE

In full view you disappear without trace,
impassive, kiss-cold, craquelure, glue,
cowrie shell without a trapped sea voice.

Unreadable text, no tics, no tells,
so when the time comes, none will know
you've seen it, rising in the hills.

Be positive. Whatever your day brings,
your lips will form a perfect O,
the first note of a wordless song.

Pilot of your own automaton,
you drift with pallid sympathy through
siege towns, riots, warzones,

fragile but illegible, until the midday
sun turns bone-ash china see-through,
reveals the inner workings of your pity.

IN CUTAWAY

Stands *me*, though it could be any of us,
sliced open, scalp to instep, en pointe
in formaldehyde inside a glass case
like some macabre Houdini stunt.

This may be a fin-de-siècle end-of-pier show,
a sicko's private gallery, a future museum
of mortality – I'd be the last to know:
dutiful sentry in cross-section,

everlasting witness to the visceral
crimson swarms that make us tick,
one open wound that will not heal.
Though I'm no escapologist, there is a trick:

I'm here, yet not here, my absence
and my presence held in stasis.
Now, step up. Place a hand on the glass.

FOR WANT OF A LEAP SECOND

our planet's spin uncouples from the time,
a lag that speeds July's arrival
before June is fully done, a crime

against chronology that leaves a hole
(though pinhead-tight) in summer
through which so much can fall:

the moment when a song is truly over,
and decay resolves as silence,
the *amen* that seals a prayer,

all syphoned through this
stolen moment with the rain
that never met the ground, the kiss

that stopped at pout, unwritten
signature, unticked box on official form,
the missing x to solve the last equation.

THE OFFSET

I set up a bad bank to protect me
from my toxic debts: the unthanked,
double-crossed, omissions and commissions.

Rows of bad tellers slump behind glass,
drumming their fingers. Sun through tall
windows crosses the spotless floor.

Bad guards play poker in the vaults
where my net worth is kept in a time-locked safe,
and non-performing assets float in jars.

In his upstairs office, my bad manager
weeps into his coffee for his lost career.
He did nothing to deserve this, poor soul.

Yet still he wears a sharp tie, keeps cut flowers,
thumbs through his empty diary, gazes out
at oblivious and solvent passers-by.

RARE SIGHTING

Because the crab apple tree is not incarnate,
but a shape cut from sky, you simply pull
its trunk a little wider and step through.

Once on the other side, you turn, take stock,
lean on a bough, and look back at it all.
So strange to catch your own life unawares,

to see your home, and those you love, move
through those rooms, lost in their own routines:
the empty semaphore of making beds,

the sacrificial steam of cooking pots;
and it looks tender, but secure, less vulnerable
than it felt when you were there, and slow.

So now, like a birder in a hide, you hold
your breath to catch yourself, out of the bath,
pausing naked at the window, staring back.

DISCOVERERS

What struck Christopher Columbus
– as his steel toecaps chipped the white
painted steps up to the citadel –

was the powder blue beneath
the white, eggshell blush below that,
flash of emerald further down.

History as layers of paint, sedimentary,
and underneath them all, spread
like a painless contagion, stone.

Beneath the stucco, pomp and limewash,
every city has a grey heart,
holds its cold within, unmoved by colour.

Not just cities either; mountains,
oceans, rainforests. It all strips back
to this. In awe he kneels and kisses it.

HYMN TO A ROLLER COASTER

Silent save the *ish* and *oss* of its rail,
the *Barracuda Backlash* runs all night,
all day for safety checks. I watch in thrall

as crash-test dummies brook their fate
unflinching, blank-masked chorus in a corkscrew
tilt at land, then sea, these belted pairs recite

a litany to sand above, to sky below,
and all around them love is played out like a line
in attic rooms, whispered into pillows.

This is the coast where humans come to pine,
on the run from work, routine and debt,
buoyed up by candyfloss and ozone.

Gravity is weaker than it should be, fate
is not enough to keep us here, tensile creatures
stretched between darkness and light.

NECESSARY AND SUFFICIENT CAUSES

The pine that falls in woods unseen
will miss the pair of magpies in a trap,

the weight of such a towering pine
will loose the cage from branch and rope,

the birds will break the canopy
and fly, for fear of life, two different routes:

the first bird to a new-built empty city,
where it marks a tyrant's statue,

the second over river, delta, strand,
out across an ever-widening strait

until it gives up any thought of land,
learns to fish, to sleep in flight,

to let itself be sculpted by the gales
into an arctic tern, to ride the countless miles,

and that, *he lied*, is why the tree must fall.

HYMN TO A GHOST TRAIN

Racketing through
plank-and-canvas caves
– sodden face-height rags,
plaster skulls on shelves,
pine disinfectant reek –
I close my eyes
and conjure tundra,
scattered reindeer,
birdless white-out skies.

A tsar's factotum,
I wax his boots against the ice,
keep his vodkas chilled.
In the carriage window, my double
glides across the endless moss;
a cold, clear spirit.

STOREHOUSES

I say of the wind: *nothing is in it.*
You hear, take hurt, the world falls still:
seas turn to float-glass, power stations prop
the sky with classical white colonnades,
city streets empty in deadening heat,
leaves hang unaware of any but themselves,
since nothing gathers them to sibilance.
Our traps are set – sheets pegged on lines,
doors left primed to slam – no sign.
You take back utterance, from sigh to hurricane,
lock it in your storehouses.

I press my ear against their corrugated
metal walls and hear each word I now can never say.
I mouth a wish: *He calls up mist from the ends*
of the earth, pulls opens rifts for rain, o breath . . .

WHAT THE BODY CANNOT HOLD

I regard myself as – *let's say* – Tokyo:
familiar yet other, secure yet shaken,
with a soul no longer inner and essential,
– not some copper thread that runs through
every vein and holds *me,* keeps me of a piece –

instead, spirit as lucent conurbation,
a city ill-defined by parks, plaques, boulevards,
but found in multiples of touch, think, speak.
Sit with me under flowering cherries,
now, in Spring, their blossom-heads

are fine-tuned instruments to pick up
every subtle shift: a falling out of love,
a tilt from youth to age. And all my cells
are cities too; stand under lime, palm, elm
in Vilnius, Krakow, Cairo, meet me there.

ON THE TILES

We could walk in now, where radiators
still tick on the walls, and terracotta
tiles take on a spill-and-footfall patina,
where windows hold firm in the sun's glare,

yet this is the floor where the women
were stripped and shaved, the men beaten, cut.
Inventory: chairs stacked, pipes still hot,
no hairlines in the walls, all tiles unbroken.

We could stand a minute's silence for each
victim, and run out of days. Eyes to shoes,
we trace the lines of grout between the rows,
the tessellated beauty of a blank mosaic,

and somewhere, among the geometric planes,
in the flat mathematics of a tiler's plans,
there must be patterns we can comprehend.

THE WOUNDS I

Betrayal begins at home, a fine-boned fledgling,
blown-in through your window, heart a-shiver.

Suffering starts out there, in vast untended forests,
where it rolls, gathers under leaves until

the day you come to find it.
Wounds are local, particular. Even his;

the man I found on wasteland out
beyond the house-backs, in a clench of gorse

too tight for dens or dogging, hangs
like a haunch amid the yellow blooms, the thorns,

the smell of coconut, his clothes ripped on re-entry,
bleached silk like a tattered parachute, his skin

dried out by wind and sun, and there,
above his eyes (still open) blood-lines

stripe his brow.

SUMMER PRAYER

O sleepless one, the sky is decked
with cloud, alas, for weeks, so all
our thoughts are overcast and sluggish.

We ride trains in hunt of sun, in vain.
Hartstongue and bracken rot in standing water,
wet roads stretch in brutal clarity.

Oceans, we suppose, still crash on
distant shingle. Landlocked, we see portents
in a clump of trackside wire, shattered

cities on the news. Even here in the head,
the heart, the body itself a sign
of distant past and rapid future.

Fast is the pulse in the unseen sun,
the unwitnessed blooms. Shadowless, unmarked,
we wait for the sun lord to break cover.

OLYMPUS

I'm given hind's feet, set on a summit,
all stumble in stranger's shoes,
wilded without warning.

Is this punishment or test?
The sun is merciless,
old gods gone to grass in foreign cities.

I pick through one-use barbecues,
beer-cans, ribs, kebab sticks.
Power thrills the wires above.

Miles below, in the valley where
I vanished mid-sentence,
mid-stride, a crowd divides my clothes,

my pockets drawn like viscera.
A dog steals my one good boot,
runs headlong into myth's damp woods.

HOW TO RAISE THE DEAD

Words will not charm me from the open casket,
serpentine and limber, loosening my maw
the better to bring you bulletins from outer space.

And your question? It's much too late to ask it.
Will you get an answer from this face of wax?
Thumbs-up from an inert unfurled claw?

If there is a way, it must require huge pressure,
immeasurable heat, primal forces of creation,
skull-cleaving noise, tectonic shifts.

But the morning lies as cold and clear as ever,
hoar frost represents the dull streets as a gift,
the air alive with love and commerce,

I'm cross-hatched with your texts, calls, prayers,
yet none will wake me. Before I petered out
I felt a pang of hunger: *herring, olives, bread, salt, oil.*

A NOTE ON THE SIDEBOARD

I must run from this, before this runs away with me,
I made a list of what I cannot lose, and now I see

that all of it will vanish if I do not step away.
Across the kitchen see this note in context: *New Year's Day*,

or rather, first day of the rest of yours and mine, the frost
has fixed the fragile world outside the glass against a loss.

The stove still warm from breakfast, a recycled envelope
(I could not find a card that showed the right amount of hope)

propped against the fruit bowl like a letter from the bank,
I realise now it doesn't name the one it needs to thank.

I try to picture heaven full, and hell an empty vault,
but all I see are leafless woods and highways sown with salt.

Turn the paper over and score out my printed name.
Leave this message on the sill and watch it fade. *No shame.*

But I must run from this, before it runs away with me.

ABYSS OF BIRDS

It begins in song, in fact in songs, such chaos
it's as if each dead bird is reborn to join
the same dawn chorus: all those shot, mauled,
window-blind, the roadkill, those whose
gist gave out in mid-migration, those whose
picking at the dry soil drew a blank, now caught
in one tremendous rinse and swoon of multiples
then down the song stoops circling and the tone
slides from tin to wood to stone it tips into
the vortex of its making, a sheer weight
of song too great to hold still and the birds
themselves are sucked in with it, corkscrew
curl of down, crop, tail and crest until it all
collapses into one dun thrush, a dusk yard,
cherry bough, a single note swells in its gullet.

THE WOUNDS II

Somebody is after me,
gaining miles a day,

and unlike me
they never stop to sleep.

I have to save this fallen pilot
before I am lost myself.

I spend hours in his gorse cell,
asking him which war,

which world, which side,
but he says nothing.

I have tried to salve the bullet-hole
in his left hand

but cannot staunch it,
rain drips off his tunic.

I set a fire to ward the foxes off.

THE FOREIGNERS

I may not admit it, but when the year tilts
to the cold, I think about them.

Their faces braille across the ones I love,
their coats slump on the back of my door.

When I'm tired, my tongue begins to form
their syllables, my fingers tap their tunes.

I find, instinctively, I turn towards the coast
forgetting the desire paths of my past.

Then I'll walk the sea wall, sit alone
in harbour cafés till my tea grows skin

and all the while I cannot picture them,
not fully, just odd details: bass oak notes

of perfume on their necks, shirts of felt,
a sense that their red is not mine, my green

not theirs, though I have never met them.

DESERT HERMITS

High noon. A resting actor hunts down
his demons in the pool, but every one
he grabs he loses. Perhaps, he thinks,
it's nothing more than his own shadow
on the pool-tiles, electrified by sun on water.

Sprinklers comb like peacocks on the lawns.
His hounds come for a soak,
then slump back to the shade of fake rocks.
If this is not a dark night, he says
to his soul, *then I don't know one.*

Out on the sand, a wild-west film-set bakes,
abandoned. Tumbleweed takes root as trees.
Night and day, yet absolutely elsewhere,
this town's shoot-outs play to lonely
salesmen in hotel rooms. *Bang.*

O SONG

O man of sorrows, I missed you
as you passed me in the street last night.
The wind funnelled between buildings,
blew grit into my eyes, fine sand
miles from the sea. *I am so sorry.*

I stopped to blink, and saw a bloom
of damson on your linen shirt,
a swarm of scarabs on your brow,
a staggered gait, as if your boots
were not a fit. I knew then it was you,

and watched you turn to look at me,
to brush your hand across my head,
a palm still wet with rain or blood.
You said some words I didn't catch,
left me lost and shot with longing.

OUT OF THE DEPTHS

have I cried unto you because no pearl diver
has ever gone so far on one held breath
beyond the seals and filaments of sun
past submarines and oil-rig footprints
threaded portholes iceberg wounds
from twilight to true darkness down
my torch fails now my camera floods
and sink to lower midnight sea's abyss
where sight begins to come back
fish ablaze with their own blush and bloom
plunge into trenches less mapped
than the solar system none come back from here
no coming up for air the water barely molten
and the vast weight of the world
borne on the tail-flick of a tint-less fish.

THE WOUNDS III

O pilot, will I ever know
what brought you down?

I pull his right glove off
and find a deeper wound.

Did this hand flinch
in fellow-feeling for the other,

upturned like a shucked crab,
legs curled in on its agony?

His cupped hand holds
a catch of blood and rain.

Fugitive and parched,
I drink from it,

and all this ersatz world,
its coincidence and chaos,

feels inevitable, utter.

ASLEEP IN THE BACK

It's dark, by which I mean it's clear enough
to see this child's head rest against
the window, but not to recognise the face.

Each time the car receives the momentary
sunrise of a streetlamp, we lean in to get
a proper look at her or him.

Emptiness of road suggests the small hours,
or a place that no one wants to go,
at least, no one save this family.

We look beyond the child's cool brow
at seeming miles of jackal-hunted scrub,
or frozen forest paths that must be kept to.

You may place one object in that hand:
pen, gun, rabbit's foot; what's it to be?
The car speeds up as dawn approaches.

TO BE READ ON ARRIVAL

It blazes. You will need no coat.
Nor maps, no point. The territories
you felt as loss were gain, the trees
they axed regrown, no route

is marked for you, just walk,
or – why not? – drive. Simply pick
from this dazzling row of classic
coupes, convertibles. No keys, no locks.

Along the coast road, you will find
the herring gulls will wish to share
their catch with you. Eat raw.
Then park and lie out on the sand.

Most visitors, before nightfall,
begin to wonder where the others are.
That is why you read this on arrival.

IN CASE OF APOCALYPSE

Alone and silent we may hear them,
plots of contingency in unobtrusive places,
backs of warehouses, breaker's yards,

and this one, a field that's neither fish
nor fowl, too wet to farm, too lush to pave,
between an airport and a forest's brink,

crow-peppered, grazed by fattening sheep,
dotted with groundsel, fern and thistle
underlooked, unmanaged, feckless.

In such backwaters, our world's *plan b*
ferments, rough alchemy in sodden soil:
mud-skippers, whirligigs, china-mark moths.

Deeper, soft emerging forms of biped:
scientists, underwriters, warlords, lawyers,
lovers, loss-adjusters; parallel futures.

HYMN TO A CAR FACTORY

The sheer beauty of machines is magnified
by multiplicity: great banks of trucks,
new-minted, not yet owned, stand under flood-

lights after rain. Behind them, in the dark,
vast hangars harbour rows of robot arms,
tilted at the tail like beak-down birds. Their work,

these flightless freaks, these corvines
– who have to scavenge to survive –
is to pick at the skeletons of family sedans.

On one wall of the plant, a man gives
up his break to paint a palm-green wash
across a mural, where in a clearing lives

an uncontacted tribe that feasts on fish,
and deeper than those shoals, white lobsters
gentle in the silt, ocean-born and brackish.

to wait for make-up, limousines and calls,
to walk the streets in faux sheet rain,
to lick an extra's lipstick off your coffee cup,

to watch playbacks, to blame your agent,
to take your continuity for granted,
to wonder all along how weightless

it would feel to come to the denouement
of the plot, or sub, you're playing in,
to stride into your own obligatory scene

– face-off with arch-antagonist –
to say your lines, to trample flowers,
to dry your eyes, fold your umbrella,

to brush a hair from your lapel,
to turn, to slam the door and leave us cut,
blanked, orphaned, staring at a vacant set.

THE WOUNDS IV

Even if I could revive him
he would barely stagger,

his boots are shot through,
and the rich tan leather

blooms with ox-blood.
He is so entwined with this,

the gorse that broke his fall,
that I begin to wonder

if he crashed at all, or rather,
broke from some aberrant pod

within this bush, but where
he might have been picked off

by gaunt winter birds,
instead he grew twisted,

too heavy to move.

STRING THEORY

Exactly what depends upon this length
of twine pinned to the ceiling (remnant
of a long-forgotten leaving do) nobody knows.

It hangs in a gape of wall-length glass
in this abandoned finance house. The place
was stripped bare, floor-by-floor, when

bets went sour, and work-stations were lost
to crates and sacks, bailiffs packed up chairs,
screens blanked, water-coolers calcified.

If only they had paid some heed to this
jute pendulum, tipped with a scrap of balloon,
had noted how the draughts and mood-swings

made it tick and feather, because, yes,
this was the instrument, calibrated
to perfection, quivering with the future.

HYMN TO A HURRICANE BOOTH

I feed it coins, step in, slide shut the glass.
I'm in here to be blown away – *120 kph of fun!*
Press GO. My coat bucks like a paper dragon,
hands braced on the walls until, unheralded,
the storm stills and holds me in its eye:

Pulse loosens, deepens to a bass drum,
and outside the booth the world accelerates:
shops change hands, close down, the mall streams
tail-light trails from days, months, years.
My kids point, laugh, then jitter, grow and leave.

If my heart could race it would, but no,
I'm silk passed through the tempest's eye
and though I know my money buys a minute
this feels like a lifetime's reckoning.
I vow to change, then step out into silence.

MONKEY GODS

They mean no harm and did not wish to be here,
but were conjured one-by-one when spells
were mistaken for jokes and told in cellar bars
or queues at tram stops. No one laughed,

but as each punchline dropped, a twist
of simian was loosed: an ear twitch, spindle finger,
show of teeth. Lamp-posts shook as we walked by.
In spite of rain and cold, this northern city

teems with them; masters of parkour
too quick to catch, cursed for pockets picked,
fruit half-bitten, hair pulled, footings lost.
Memento-mischief, where do you go at sunset?

We trapped one in the rafters of a disused mill
and tied it up until it told us what it knew.
We cut its throat and swore to keep our counsel.

SOUL SONG

The countless pinprick points of light
that make us human also map us,
so if I looked at you in love, complete

in utter darkness, I would see
a swarm of fireflies, carriers
of every half-formed thought, your history,

and with each breath and kiss
your filigree of sparks would cloud
and cross with mine, except of course

no room is ever night enough, no dark
can be so utter as to let us see this.
But feel the hairs lift on your neck,

that static charge, and know that we
have met our souls, invisible but physical,
akin to gale force, thunder, gravity.

DARK NIGHT OF THE SOUL

Last street in the furthest town before
the desert: perfect rows of terracotta
villas backing onto empty. Nights
are hard in these box bedrooms,
worn down by the weight of nothing.

These homes change hands by the year,
since none can stand the sleepless hours,
the vapids, stock-still in bed as the tiles
tick and cool. Backyards are crossed
by the slow morse of floodlights. Geckos

skitter on the roof where gutters atrophy.
A gate swings, though there is no wind.
Locks loosen without key or cause.
In high-rise towers on the morning side
of earth, numbers rise and fall on screens.

THE ROAD RETAKEN

Walking backwards into the desert, your neck aches
from its owl-swivel and your calves and ankles seize.

You divest yourself of gadgets and accoutrements,
then garments, naked for a while until the hair

crops up all over. Reversing through suburbs you
bump into signs, parked cars. Some truck near wings you,

and its driver gives a finger and a blast. So, out
past flower-sellers, fields, then dirt-tracks, cutting up

your heels, you crouch, hunch, pass the final fruit stall,
tidy filling station, hitch-hikers with cardboard signs,

the shouts and jeers become incomprehensible to you,
keep on is all, until your ragged toes touch sand.

You have forgotten all you ever knew: books, doctrines,
symphonies; whole cultures are unwritten. That hot breeze

tastes of nothing. Turn round. Drop to all fours. Now run.

HYMN TO THE FALSCHFAHRER

To the rider who tears to the end of a slip road

(not because he hairpins into the teeth of the flow,
to the rhythm of tilt and counter-tilt between
oncoming cars, a compass needle twitching north
but on the southbound carriageway;
not because he takes his ride at night without lights,
nor because it sings of salmon's upstream rush,
– he is not heading for the source of road,
some tarmac spring up in the hills, *not that* –
but simply because he is a seeker after friction,
winding back the old road so his wheels coil
tighter, tauter, then with all his muster
coiled and held he turns, kicks down, and powers
into the future, pulling us in tailwind after)

to him and his machine be praise, hallow, traction.

DELIVER US THIS

Set out a table, o vengeful one, in sight
of our enemies, so we can revel
in the victory we have not as yet sealed.

Let us plan our menu by the rule of opposites:
the filthier their water, the sharper our vodka,
the more their bread mottles

with blue rosettes, the more pursed
their fruit . . . *You get the gist.* Set a spread
on a roof garden in their oldest city,

so we can cast down crusts and oyster-shells,
watch them scrabble, fight and beg.
Then when the banquet's done,

let us walk down among them,
look them in the eyes, memorise the tics,
the tongues that make them less than us.

THE WOUNDS V

Those who pursue me
are mere hours away.

Where they come from,
there is no rain,

so their tyres smell
of cinder tracks and tar.

I wince at the sound
of an engine, slam of a door.

I cannot save this pilot,
not with such a loss of blood.

So I rip his shirt to bare
the largest wound,

beneath his ribs. I tear
the wound lips wider still,

climb inside and hide.

LACHRIMA NEGATIVA

Someone told me not to cry,
and since that day tears fail me,
hard before they form and fall,

seeds between thumb and finger,
flies' eggs on a tear duct's rose,
too sore now to rub.

Still the tides turn and swell
behind my eyes, but on the cheekbones'
strand they wash up only silt,

grit, some sour amber sugar.
Whose fault is this drought?
I recall a crowded street:

carnival, market stalls, cooking smells,
dry lips that brushed my ear.
Someone told me not to cry.

IN BABYLON

We hang our harps in trees
and will not sing. It's fine, we say,
since the songs are so old no one
will forget their tunes. Besides,
they play them all day on the radio.

This much is true. Except
the blast de-tuned the wirelesses,
and all they do is jabber now,
plus spring's rise in the river
gave the willow roots a rush

and our harps grew out of reach.
One day, like typist monkeys,
breeze and leaves will stumble on
our songs, but for now this desperate
acappella is our only praise, *o, o, o.*

TO AN IMMORTAL I

The first deaths you suffered
– slave-ships, blazing tenements,
monsoon flash-floods, plagues –

must have left you with a hangover,
a sense of semi-presence, guilt
that you got what you wished for.

No one warned you that this after-half
meant deathless, not invulnerable,
and you have lost so many loved,

have known and seen such harm,
so now you seek out half-thawed lakes,
high balconies, to flirt with it.

For you alone, I make an offering,
you who have heard it all before,
I give you this, my mortal song.

HOUND-GOD

In the pantheon of standby gods,
a place is kept for this stray bitch,
a-scavenge in a border town.

Each time she sleeps,
the world loops on
another thousand years.

She wakes, expecting:
litters, suckles, whelps, then bites
their heels until they make

their own way in the wild.
Nobody knows it
but she keeps her town in

water, cool and sweet as nectarine.
In case of dire need,
you may use this silent whistle.

IN PRAISE OF FLAKING WALLS

To be alive is to throw shadows.
No mere ghost could obstruct the light
like we do. This much we know:

that to be made incarnate
is to be as solid as this limewashed wall,
to come from rumour, hope, to weight.

We know that sheets of stucco crumble
under frost and sun, that every flaw
is nailed by lichen, that all

this is provisional. We know more:
that such beautiful distress – a stone
wall turned to mud and straw –

will be mirrored in our own,
that mountains will give way to snow,
that light will look through us again.

IN PRAISE OF THE PRESENT

If being here and now is nothing more
than memory on the fly, then love
is just a trace of having loved, over

and over-recorded, so each new
detail – that lock of hair that mimes
your cheekbone's curve, those blue

ghost-maps beneath cream skin –
becomes a vivid present, and a fix,
a holding fast, a living in

not after. This I pledge: to stay
awake, for death can keep its dreams.
Here is enough, and now, time's alchemy.

So put your book down, it's so late.
I lean in close and say your name,
to print it on the face of night.

A CROSSING

To those who knew one side alone,
it seemed another life,
the far bank of an iced canal.

First step, a shift of weight so slow
that even thawed it may not fail.
You leave twin trails of skid-steps.

Across, you rise into a place
of ghosted ash trees, cream-hide
gentle cattle, slo-mo like blank manatees.

Call a name you love, and hear
your voice as you have never known it,
like the pulse of a skein in flight.

To those whose eyes are ever open
world can offer this: a frozen threshold
crossed, a cutting-loose, a loss.

FOOTFALL

In the minutes after birth, when midwives
do their weighing, swaddling, when they
hand you to your mother for your first suck,
all your shoes line up outside the room:

tiny soft-cloth purses, straight-laced
school brogues, one-night pairs you hired
for bowling, ice-skates, thigh boots, killer heels,
right through to soft again - misshapen slippers.

There is mercy in this moment,
so fleeting that your mother, father, never walk
the line, nor see it falter into sole-holed poverty,
or stop halfway with an immaculate stiletto.

Besides, you cannot read the runes from shoes.
You might become an actor, a dictator, barefoot
centenarian, a rumour, a ghost, a name in a book.

CORPOREAL

Thrown by their shadows
into pale upstanding citizens,
stride down their sundry streets
the incarnate, who though

outnumbered by the dead
have over them the rush of may
in bloom and starling dusk-songs,
stone beneath their shoes

not slabbed above them,
all the fear and fury of the bodied
– cuts, burns, lips, fingers –
and countless acts of love

that must be used in full
and well because they weigh
too much to leave the world.

THE VOWS

We pledge to wake each morning face-to-face,
to shun the orders of the busy sun,
we promise to disturb each other's peace.

And we will, yes, gaze at the pining moon,
will pick out brine-blown glass-gems from the strand,
will read our future scratched onto a stone.

We both believe that silence turns to sand
and promise not to add to the unsaid,
we meet here as the raging sea meets land.

We want the risen life before we're dead,
our passion will be squandered more than spent,
we hereby swear to spend our days in bed.

We're naked, till we wear each other's scent
and recognise it quicker than our own.
You start and finish me, you're my extent.

IT IS COMING

Our youngest and hardiest may live to see
the people of the future take over our streets,
homes, parks, and they are not like us.

Knowing as they do that bodies,
like old glass, are ultra-viscous liquids,
they have mastered constant motion

lest they slip through their own fingers.
Hairstyles change, and jokes.
They find our humour charming.

Watch them smoking without harm,
strolling down your hallway to cook dishes
never conjured in your kitchen.

If this is you, then hang your head,
see how you make us feel,
how you devalue all we thought we had.

AQUA FREAKSHOW

Between the firefish and the conger eels,
your life suspended here in water.
Too many spectators, come back later,
after-hours when filter motor's all

you hear, then stand, head bowed,
before your span, a hank, kebabed,
turned in the artificial tide,
your sum, your soul, your mother-lode.

You watch the water loose life's hold
upon itself, as strands peel off
revealing naked wounds of love,
your years, like white fat, marbled

on the raw reds of your terror,
keep watching, as your life diffuses,
how the lightest meat makes up the core.

TO AN IMMORTAL II

Once I got my eye in it was easy
to know your kind in crowds:
a studied at-home-ness, skin as hide,

clothes worn as costume,
tiredness borne in the bones.
See it once, you know it every time.

And even if I can't be certain,
all I do is ask you for a match,
and in that momentary flame

I watch the silent shadow-play
of all you've witnessed
printed on your retinas.

I should know not to go with you;
your nakedness a map of cuts,
fingerprints worn smooth.

PORTRAIT OF THE PSALMIST IN
UTTER DARKNESS

Not his absence, not his finding himself
wept up on some far shore, leaving here
an empty frame, life story with hole-in-the-heart,

this portrait is left intentionally blank
so you can add your own king, hero, waste-of-space,
a legend in the local sense alone, perhaps,

a question where the answers should have been,
a heap of clothes draped on a throne, bent crown,
a locked, un-windowed, silent room.

On trust we take the presence of a man,
the fact that he is crying still, his hands held
out to us in desperate supplication,

but this anti-incarnation need not keep us,
not when you turn aside and see the glory
of the lit now, then smell it on your fingers.

WETSALTER

So here's the rub: his salt, your skin.
He flays you first, then kneads it in,

he hooks you up in smokehouse dark
then turns you till you meet his mark,

hacks you down and cuts you loose,
neck is raw where flesh met noose,

but cured you are, prosciutto-man
your self preserved in perma-tan,

you walk the streets and haunt the bars,
drink too much and drive fast cars,

one woman falls for you and weeps,
she holds you as your slab-self sleeps,

her tears betray the stakes, the cost,
your meat preserved, your mojo lost.

She tells you. This is your riposte . . .

A NEW SONG

Sing a new song to the Lord,
sing through the skin of your teeth,
sing in the code of your blood,
sing with a throat full of earth,

sing to the quick of your nails,
sing from the knots of your lungs,
sing like a dancer on coals,
sing as a madman in tongues,

sing as if singing made sense,
sing in the caves of your heart,
sing like you want them to dance,
sing through the shades of your past,

sing what you never could say,
sing at the fulcrum of joy,
sing without need of reply.

THE DEFENESTRATIONS

of Prague were just the start of it, now everything
is falling, in a cloudburst from high windows
down past mine, and out of mine past those below.
My eyes, accustomed to the downward tow,
cannot fix on a face these days, but slide to shoes
as if in constant shame, and my declivity of gazing
anticipates the drop of leaves before they fall.

As yet, I have not felt drafted, called or marked
though most of my belongings took a plummet.
A few of us refuseniks gather here in my bare flat
to learn songs of ascent and try to slow the cataract
but there is such a grace, a beauty to it all,
that now I catch myself entranced by lemons, dresses,
bottles, chairs, lamps, books beguiled by gravity,
obedient and true to earth, though I would not confess it.

THE RIND

World is not raw enough, not nearly,
so you sit in the kitchen and peel it
with your fingers. Over-ripe, it stains
your hands orange, and the discarded

rind curls on the table like Antarctica,
like Africa, leaving in your palm
an orb of ambergris, off-white,
moist and guile-less, bird-in-hand.

Not naked enough, not even now,
so world is split between your thumbs
along its fault-lines, broken into islands,
each one burst against your palate.

Take care, o man-who-ate-the-world,
because your skin gives you away:
perfume of midday sun, cloves, zest.

BATHSHEBA'S PUZZLE

Although she does not know about the others,
this sometime beauty, bather, lover sits
on the edge of her bed now and looks out
across the roofscape of her city until (over

whelmed with tiredness) she lies back,
feet on floorboards, halfway between
sit and lie, and stares up at the stain
that spreads across her ceiling (old leak

unrepaired and rust-brown) till its shape
reminds her of a scorpion, storm cloud,
some rare hieroglyph. If only she could read
this message from the skies (a sign of hope,

that elements should bother) she would
know the truth, and across the rain-marked world
another woman does this, and another, and a third.

JETSAM

Somewhere, on an island's blasted north coast,
fishermen are circling a body on the beach,
washed up with net-floats, buoys and rope.

It seems at first to be a basalt outcrop,
off-cast spare tyre from a monster truck,
a half-set heap of tarmac miles from roads,

but close up, it turns velveteen, its shape
plumped out by unseen ribs and spine, a full tail
ploughed into the sand, a fly-blown mound

with gashes in each side from gull-beaks
and the spray, yet though they look and poke
the locals cannot find its eyes, *cannot*.

Though we live worlds away we find our lives
more graceful, agile now. For years that thing
has held us like a grudge in ocean trenches.

ASCENSION

A picture of restraint, he stands in the corner of a bar,
in blackout coat, fedora, false beard and his eyes shut.
He speaks to no one, points and nods to get his drinks.
The stakes are high. If he lifts a lid, or lets a coat
lapel fall open: blinding blue! So he holds tight.

Who would guess that after millions of nights
behind the gem-encrusted curtain, day-sky itself
has come down in the dark hours, to see how
we get by without it. And how? Music helps us,
dancing, drink. Electricity animates our phantom days.

At closing time he tries to say goodnight, but lets fly
a fusillade of birdsong. Stepping out, a button slips
and from his coat breaks ether, azure, ultramarine,
in a blinding daylight flash. Next morning,
he is back in place; there must have been a kind of rise.

FROM THE DEAD

Today fish come back to a world
robbed of fins, scales, the o-gape.
I used to think that they would boil,

oceans over-brim and steep
in herring, tuna, cod, shark, plaice,
waters stitched with dives and leaps.

Instead, it grows from silence
in the silt bed of a frozen lake,
unwitnessed tipping of the balance.

Lake thickens into slick, takes
up its sinew, gristle, as if water's
own body is the one come back,

as if a shoal is what a body was,
and soul the endless electrical
tracery of all our love and impulse.

SONG OF ASCENT

Conjure this: true rise is
not a thinning into weightlessness,
some shimmer of a desert road's
horizon, nor the tranquil lift
of chinese lanterns, but

an act of muscle, guts,
against the odds and grain,
a full reversal of the planet's
sacred pull, a heavy-booted,
deep-snow-footed tail-turn

in which trees take up
their roots and walk,
where streets up-strip and peel,
and you, eyes wide, in waiting
for a *go* that will not come.

DISCOVERERS

What foxed Ferdinand Magellan as his fingers
traced the coastlines, sandbanks, dragon-backs,
was how his charts did not map what he saw,

and this the first leg of a loop around the globe,
would take him from Atlantic through Pacific
out across the dark back of the earth's face,

so he burned the charts, listened to the strains
of the voices in his head, primeval echoes
of an old illiterate God, like mollymawk cries.

The more he heard, the more he understood
this was his elegy, a call-and-response which he
must learn by heart until he nailed it every time.

This, and only this, would get them home,
not the astrolabes and cross-staffs, so he let
the *Trinidad* float free, and sang his antiphon.

TO AN IMMORTAL III

Our turn now, so order obeys:
moons and planets glide and lock
into alignment around us, our days

line up to point to this one night,
worlds pivot on one narrow alley, rain,
a distant siren. *Alright,*

so immortals make bad lovers,
too jaded, incapable of tenderness,
fingers tempered by too many others.

But why does the sky pull
into an orrery around our star
if there is nothing good about this fall?

I raise my shivering lips to hers
as she unbuttons me, her touch
– so sure – conducts the universe.

REFUSENIKS

Who always have their reasons,
like the girl who sent the angel packing,
kept on sewing, combing, sighing;

the city planner who turned down
those hanging gardens, that colossus,
he who stuck to his grid come hell

or the ferryman at high water
holed-up in his attic bottling ships
as neighbours drowned for want of a boat.

So this time I will not say no,
when the bell rings, the shattered dove
alights on my windowsill,

the stranger puts a note through my door,
when I find, in a dream, a new room
in my house I will force the lock.

AUTOMATIC SOOTHSAYER BOOTH

Your custom is my pleasure, now look into my eyes,
Destino reads your fortune like a mortal reads a book,

I cannot be held liable for heartbreak or surprise,
the road ahead is twisted so you may not want to look.

This turban should be ochre but will pale a shade each year,
my beard was once a boot brush, my cloak a velvet drape,

I come not from the mystic east but from a cold north pier,
my utterance is orphic, my voice a loop of tape.

I'm half a man, so legless, a torso on a plank,
my name is not *Destino*, but your own name in reverse.

Your next decade is joyful, and your wife's the one to thank,
from then on it's a nightmare, I'm sorry to be terse.

I'd make the most of winters, but stay out of the sun,
drink more milk than whisky, never race a hearse,

don't invest in futures and remember life is fun.

UNDER HIS AEGIS

The head of a king is on its way home,
to the palace where it once held sway.

Unmade roads, flint passes, old limo
with shot suspension, three young men,

idealists all, keep silence, and the head
in a steel box strapped to the back seat.

Their work was brutal, in the thin copse
where they found him lame and shivering.

They should worry what this boxed fruit
– mottled with bruises and dried blood,

when they lift it out to show the crowd –
might say, what incantations, provocations,

or most dangerous of all, what elegies,
what songs of walnut groves, vineyards,

colours of a childhood long since lost to us.

THE CONJURER ATTEMPTS
A FINAL TRICK

If he could list the things he's touched
in order of their music – sash, lash, calabash –
how far could he recover them,
simply by the sounding of their names?

He finds himself a house, boarded-up,
built for a boom that never came,
and in that house a room so bare, so haunted
it holds absence – fleet and fugitive – within it.

Cross-legged on the unmarked boards,
he cups his hands and says it out loud, *cash*,
weight and warmth of coin and paper,
fine-boned fistful like a broken bird.

Focus, conjure something out of nothing.
But litter skims dry streets outside, puts him off.
Mosquitos bloom and hang. *It's now or never.*

THE SEA AGAIN

has been among us in the night.
I knew it from the trace of grit
beneath my feet, salt on my tongue-root.

The very last S of the backwash
filled my ears. Yet by dawn there it was,
tame between the harbour walls.

This was not the first time.
I know how hard comes true attention:
to hold the present moment between

teeth and tongue like a snail
on a pin, its shell an inverse pearl.
And yet I will, *I will*

work out what sea could want from us
when it has all the density and poise.
I bait, with breath, an empty glass.

ANGEL OF THE ABYSS

She does not like the details, and for that deserves
no blame. She hangs back at the edge of woods
where men line up on brinks of pits they had to dig,
or on the fire escape as doors are broken down.

She smokes, not to be blasé, but to offer it as prayer.
She wears a high-viz jacket, no thick cloak or hood,
for fear of turning into her own tribute act.
At home alone lit by the TV screen she watches

sports and stand-up, skips the news, then paces
out her empty rooms, laments the allocations,
how she wound up ushering the sick or shot when
the healer, or *angel of the perfumes* would have suited.

Nonetheless, she goes where she is sent,
in trust that each last word, inaudible to all but her,
will hold together as a testament, to learn by rote.

PORTRAIT OF THE PSALMIST AS
ULTRA-SINGER

I sing for fear I'll hear the still
small voice and not like what it says,
I croon to make my skull full

as a squat hive and the honey
is my cracked song, my sting in the throat.
O I know a bee is not a melody

but I must come to terms with what
it is that leaves me hoarse
that keeps my house awake all night.

The one I love mouths *we are lost*
behind my back, which means nothing,
but this is what I fear the most.

Listen. The unsung is unuttering,
sucking back into itself,
the inverse of words, an unworn ring.

ON GRACE

The wolf at the door heads a queue
of houseflies, blowflies, mildew, mice,
rats, rain, rot, looters, taxmen.
All they need is time, or a window
left ajar. How thin, how brittle is

the carapace of all this, baulked
against the towering years. And yet,
great oaks still pivot on the toe-tips
of their shadows in a day-long pirouette,
in palace gardens no one visits.

October ripens under leaf-mould,
ancient limewashed walls grow warm
in late, slant sun. A deer halts in a field alone.
There are worlds out here to long for.
And we are not lost yet.

A PLEA FOR CLEMENCY

Quickly, come quickly, o agents of repair,
the fisher king lies wounded, fields have run to wrack,
woods are choked with frostbite, sun can barely rise,
hungry curs are hunting, feral in their packs,
quickly, come quickly, o agents of repair.

Quickly, work quickly, o engines of repair,
cars have come to gridlock, air is thick with flies,
oligarchs and spin-men peer through tinted glass,
the price of parts has risen, a run on teeth and eyes,
quickly, work quickly, o engines of repair.

Quickly, go quickly, o agents of repair,
balance good and evil on your subtle calculus,
stitch and salve the wounded, salt and sow the ice,
then slip away in darkness, so no one sees you pass,
quickly, go quickly, o agents of repair.

THE ORDER

She slid a chest beneath her childhood bed,
collecting for the day she set up home:
bequests, birthdays, every coin she spared

would go to buy a candle, cup, a spoon.
She kept them separate: silver, linen, plate,
curator of her future life's museum.

She married, mothered, held her household tight,
surrounded by the objects she had saved.
She kept the drawers and shelves immaculate.

Then one spring day they ordered her to leave.
She packed what she could carry in that chest.
The train was cramped; her children silent, brave.

And now her things are ordered like the rest:
a cloche of knives and forks, a room of boots,
a plait of fading hair behind lit glass.

PETITION

What do we want (we cursers in cars, queuing
in hope to get out of the city – cases stuffed
with papers purporting to represent money –
whose faces are mere fronts for re-runs, rehearsals,
who know we never truly know each other,

let alone ourselves, who will not let ourselves alone,
but worry solace till it shrugs off, whose radios
make weightless objects of words – bleak bulletins
from somewhere else – who have a bad song snagged
inside and mouth it to get rid, while roadside limes,

a boulevard let's say, bow in steep rain to form
an arch triumphal for this solemn urban exit, past
colonnaded cafés running dry, shops in hock,
windows fly-posted to sell some gig or *change-your-life*,
who call ahead to warn the kids) from you?

THE END OF CIVILISATION
AS WE KNOW IT

Right now, a hound dreams on a porch
overlooking endless desert. No one can tell
the content of his dreams, but watching
we might wonder – from the flicker
of his eyelids – if he sees a jack-rabbit squat
by the scrub's edge, taut and taunting him,
spring-loaded, or the pulse in his haunches
means a hurtle down a long straight road
behind his man's accelerating pickup.
But what if these are mere nerve tics,
without cause or meaning, and the dream
is less a story than a place, less place than state,
an openness through which the wilderness
will pour itself, a foothold, first step to our towns,
our homes, the crack that lets the desert in.

HYMN TO A KARAOKE BOOTH

A monk's cell, a hostel, a place where lovers
come to meet (who should not meet) a lush
chintz boudoir trimmed in gold, huge-eyed
paste lions grinning from each corner,
wide screen with a thousand songs inside,
two glasses, microphones switched on.

The booth croons *I wanna fall from the stars.*
We pause the song to talk. So stellar are you
that I fear I see an ancient light (your dress
a cover of a sixties hit) the true of you long-dead,
the distant heart's blaze long extinguished.

We need some kind of test to check if this
is real – a kiss, a touch of hair, an answered prayer –
but burnt into the locked screen warns the song:
you will never never never know me.

THE MIRROR TEST

They bring us, one by one, to face the glass,
having marked us each with black ink crosses
on the cheek. First bonobos pass, orangutans,

then elephants and magpies, self-awareness
vivid in their angst about this new scar,
testing it with tongue, trunk, wing. Me now.

I stare into a temperate and muted world,
wall with posters in a foreign script,
tall windows, mountains rising to a coast.

And in the middle of that other room,
a man is buttoned up inside a woman's coat,
his face marked like mine for some unstated sin,

but on the other cheek. He pities me,
leans in as if to speak, but before a word is said
they fail me, send me back into the jungle.

FRAGMENTS INTO WORLD

A note resolves, hum becomes chime,
the floor stirs and broken moon is combed
from shattered sun in utter darkness.

Then like wrong rain it falls up, gathers in the sky.
Sunlit now, we see the devastation, watch
as windows heal and pull together, towers,

palaces, museums rear up dripping
from the dry sea of themselves,
forests fan like spines from sharp seeds,

then the details: clock-faces turn limpid,
cups and mirrors form and seal,
a recapitulation of the world we knew.

So once again we walk, and witness,
give thanks for the tangible and visible,
but no one dares to sing a note, dig in a heel.

ACKNOWLEDGEMENTS

Acknowledgements are due to the editors of the following:

Guardian, Guernica, Image, London Review of Books, Magma, Manchester Review, New Welsh Review, Poem, PN Review, Poetry Ireland Review, Poetry London, Poetry Review, Port, Rialto, Temenos.

A number of these poems have been broadcast in drama and feature strands on BBC Radio 3 and Radio 4.

The poems linked to the vision of 'Hotel Splendide' were commissioned by the Manchester Literature Festival, performed as part of a concert by the Manchester Camerata, and broadcast on Medici TV.

'The Order' was commissioned by the CCJ for Holocaust Memorial Day.

'Mene, Mene, Tekel, Upharsin' was commissioned for the book *Crrritic*, published by Sussex Academic Press.